GRUNEWALD

The World's Masters – New Series

by Anthony Bertram

THE STUDIO PUBLICATIONS, LONDON & NEW YORK

FIRST PUBLISHED 1950

WORLD'S MASTERS NEW SERIES *Editor: ANTHONY BERTRAM*

The covers of this series, designed by Arthur Hundleby, are based on heraldic motives representing the national school to which each artist belongs or with which he is chiefly associated

Already published

WILLIAM BLAKE

SANDRO BOTTICELLI

JAN VERMEER OF DELFT

HANS HOLBEIN THE YOUNGER

WILLIAM HOGARTH

JEAN AUGUSTE DOMINIQUE INGRES

PIERO DELLA FRANCESCA

EL GRECO

MICHELANGELO

PIETER BRUEGEL

EUGENE DELACROIX

HIERONYMUS BOSCH

THE VAN EYCKS

Others in preparation

Printed in Great Britain by William Clowes & Sons Ltd, London and Beccles. Published in London by The Studio Ltd, 66 Chandos Place, WC2, and in New York by the Studio Publications Inc, 381 Fourth Avenue

Introduction

WE know nothing substantial of the man we call Grüne-wald. We are not even sure of his name: it was probably Mathis Gothart, surnamed Nithart and Grünewald. We know nothing of his origins or apprenticeship, his opinions or associates; we but imperfectly know where he was active, except that he seems never to have left the area of the Middle Rhine. There is one glimpse of him in the gossipy account of German painters which Joachim von Sandrart published fifty years after his death. Sandrart is unreliable, but this item may have come from some old man's memory, and it rings true: 'He led a lonely and melancholy life, and was unhappily married.' ('Ein eingezogenes Leben geführt, und übel verheuratet gewesen.')

It was only at the beginning of this century that Grünewald's reputation began, even in Germany, to grow towards its present eminence, as that of one who stands with Dürer and Holbein in the top rank of German painters. The interest in him since 1914 is strikingly indicated by Burkhard's bibliography. (See Bibliographical Notes.) And now *The Times Literary Supplement* (18 September, 1948) can write of his work as 'the expression of a personal ecstacy which his two famous contemporaries could not have aspired to experience'. I believe this is true; but his work, of course, has not the scope of Dürer's nor the precision of Holbein's. If he stands beside them, it is for his own qualities, and not as a rival of theirs.

He was not a prolific artist. Burkhard's catalogue admits only

3

twenty-three panels and thirty-three drawings as authentic. Of the panels, nine belong to one work, the Isenheim altarpiece; and the definite and probable relationships of others reduce the number of separate altarpieces to some ten or eleven. The tireless examination of records in recent years has only revealed the identity of four lost works. His themes are even more restricted in number. Nine panels —over a third of his output—are concerned with the Passion. No secular subject survives; nor is there any trace of his ever having painted one. Nothing in his work but an occasional architectural background suggests that the humanism of the Renaissance had any effect on him whatsoever. But that is not peculiar to him. The Renaissance in Germany was almost exclusively a religious movement. It is the cases of Dürer and Holbein that are exceptional, and it was not in Germany that they were influenced to break away from the Gothic. But neither does Grünewald seem to have been affected by the Reformation, although there is one fragment of evidence that he may have been interested in it: a New Testament in German and certain Lutheran works were found in a nailed-up chest that had belonged to him. But the whole tenor of his works weighs against our interpreting that as meaning more than interest.

We may conclude, then, that his faith and philosophy were essentially Gothic. But in two ways he was a man of his time: in his realism and in his sense of space. He handled space like a romantic. It is not a defined space, like that of the Italian Renaissance, but an infinite and mysterious space. 'The indescribable power of space in his *nights*', said Oswald Spengler, 'is equalled only by Rembrandt.' But they are not nights: they are something more terrible and more subjective—the experience of a day when there was a darkness over all the earth. In the Small Crucifixion (Plate xxxiii) the

4

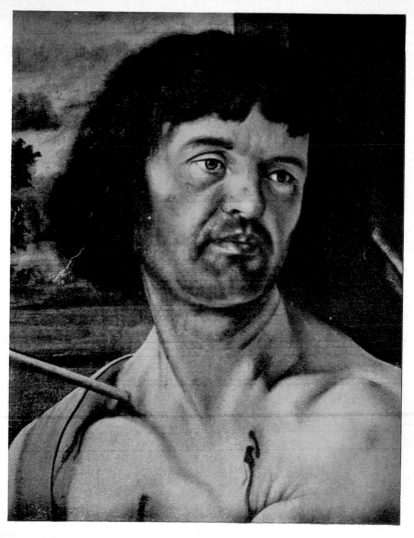

SELF-PORTRAIT OF THE ARTIST (?) AS ST SEBASTIAN. Detail from Plate XVIII.

shrivelled sun above the cross is in almost total eclipse. It is so far away that the petty astronomical measured space is overwhelmed; but the figures are not, and it is this, their capacity to stand up large against such a scale of space, that gives them their mystic power. The realism of their handling, that might have pulled them down to the mere measure of earth, transcends itself by this showing of them as immense in an infinite space.

Indeed, the characteristic greatness of Grünewald lies in his reconciliation of scientific realism with religious ecstacy—a reconciliation which can only take place outside measurable time and space. But this scientific realism in the painting of a tortured body and stricken spirits is quite the opposite to what W. H. Auden has called 'the surgeon's idea of pain.' It is not detached: it does not calculate the balance between the pain and what is bought by it; but, on the contrary, it is heavily charged with personal emotion. He feels every wound he paints.

In this emotionalism, as in his freedom in space, Grünewald was a precursor of the Baroque, the movement in European art which broke up the classic restraint of the early Renaissance and prepared the way for full-blown romanticism. He points from the Middle Ages towards El Greco and Blake, Van Gogh and the surrealists.[1]

In my limited space I can best illustrate these generalizations from one work—the stupendous Isenheim altarpiece. We shall understand his other paintings if we understand this enterprise, the largest and most elaborate altarpiece in Northern Europe; and I shall make but passing references to them.

As I have said in the introduction to *The Van Eycks* in this series, we must never forget that Northern painting derives from the

[1] See *Bosch* in this series for a definition of surrealism.

6

illuminated book: it unfolds in time. When the critic writes about a more formal art, he is hampered by his medium, which compels him to discuss in sequence what is taken in all at once by the eyes. He is less hampered in such a work as this altarpiece, which itself has a sequence. It begins, when the wings are closed, with the theme of the Passion (Plate viii). It has been suggested that Grünewald handled this dead Christ with such realism because the altarpiece was commissioned by the Antonites, an order whose hospitals were devoted to sufferers from St Anthony's fire, a skin disease related to the plague and considered incurable. Those disfigured worshippers would find consolation in a God whose torture had robbed Him also of all beauty and seemliness. But although other aspects of the altarpiece were undoubtedly influenced by its destination, this treatment of the dead Christ is common to all Grünewald's *Crucifixions* and *Pietà's*. He felt that in the depth of His suffering Christ was most completely man; and he strove, therefore, in this aspect, to make him as man-like as possible. It appears from medical opinion that he probably found his model in the hospital mortuary, as he did for the demon in the lower left corner of *The Temptation of St Anthony* (Plate xxx). In his passionate desire to make us realize imaginatively, as it were in our own bodies, what Christ suffered, he does not spare us one repellent detail, the prurient greens, the blue, swollen lips, the protruding tongue, the inflammation round each tear in the flesh, the hands crisped in agony, the arms wrenched from their sockets. Moreover, he pushes his realism also to the accessories: the rough cross, with its beam bending under the weight, the dirty and tattered loincloth, the scrap of paper on which the I.N.R.I. is crudely written, nailed on an odd piece of plank and hung on the cross, the sordid makeshift of indifferent men in a hurry—all horribly as it must have been. The truth of the early Italians who painted an

7

unbattered Christ, held aloft like a banner on a cross of fine cabinet-work, wearing a neatly plaited crown of thorns and a clean loin-cloth that curved in lyric sweeps, labelled with an inscription in exquisite lettering, all this in a pattern of clear colour against a serene gold background—the truth of this was one truth, the cele-bration of a Saviour's triumph : and the truth of Grünewald (so far as we have gone) was another truth, a bitter dirge over one who was despised and rejected.

But against all this realism—or rather, not against it, but suffusing it—is the whole mystic 'feel' of the picture. The effect is not that of a mere record, as of the death of some common criminal. An infinitely significant drama is present in the brooding sky, storm-heavy with a sombre and terrible green, against which the figures are set in a ritual solemnity. The crucifix is shifted slightly to the right of the centre, to correct the unsymmetrical placing of the assistants. This shift runs down into the predella. Everything is for-mally bound together by a rhythmic repetition of reds and whites, and by a series of inverted triangles and horizontal lines which links the whole alterpiece so that the design has the potent non-realism of a stately metrical pattern. The figure of the Baptist holds its own in the design not merely by that shifting of the centre, but also by its own massiveness and by the tremendous prophetic gesture which is echoed by that of St Sebastian in the right wing, as the position of the Evangelist's arm is by that of St Anthony's in the left. His book gives a slanting movement into the picture, which corresponds with that made by the group of the Evangelist and the Virgin. The most outstanding non-realistic elements, however, are the boldly written inscription, the Lamb of God and the Gothic disproportion of the figures. Here is no academic realist striving for illusion.

8

We can learn a great deal more about Grünewald's treatment of this theme by comparison with his other versions. We find, for example, a steady reduction in the number of assistants. The earlier Basle version (Plate vii) is overcrowded. The centurion's gesture is a relatively feeble foretaste of the Baptist's. The triangular construction is weaker and the general effect less solemn and more emotional. In the later *Small Crucifixion* (Plate xxxiii) the triangles are more acute and the impression more disturbing, more tattered and emaciated and humanly dramatic; while in the Karlsruhe version (Plate xxxiv) the forms are fuller, heavier. The crown of thorns has grown into a monstrosity: the figure of Christ hangs with a more oppressive weight of death. It is consummated. The crowd has gone: the central drama is over. The gesture of St John's tense and almost hysterical efforts to control himself is in most poignant contrast to the peasant mother, huddled in her inelegant clothes, who takes a load which will weigh on her much longer than on the sensitive, almost neurotic young man. In this, as in the preceding version, realism has taken the upper hand because the tragedy is unrelieved by the vision of the centurion or the prevision of the Baptist or the promise of the Lamb.

The tremendous event we have been discussing is, in the Isenheim altarpiece, flanked by two calm panels which offer intellectual parallels. At the sight of St Anthony we remember the violence of his temptations; at that of St Sebastian, the suffering of his martyrdom: both were faithful. Below, in the predella, Grünewald shows the sickening aftermath of sacrifice, all exultation gone, the dead body and the mourners. It is, if one may without irreverence make such a comparison, as when the body of the bull is ignominiously dragged off by horses after the consummation of the kill.

And that note sounds as a memorial of what Christ paid, even

9

when the wings are opened and we are dazzled by the incandescent and ecstatic vision of the *Incarnation* (Plate ix). In the left wing we see its annunciation. In a serene Gothic church, flooded with sunshine, Gabriel, a splendid figure in red and gold, swirls down in a turmoil of drapery—perhaps the most completely baroque figure Grünewald painted. As a supernatural being he is, it should again be noticed, out of all human proportion to the Virgin and the church. The element of realism intrudes with the detailed painting of the tiles and the domestic adjuncts of books and furniture. But in the central panel, the Incarnation itself, the mystical vision is overwhelmingly dominant, made all the more so by its absorption of the simple bath-tub, the bed and so on into this transcendant, Blake-like vision. The radiant figure of the crowned and aureoled Queen of Heaven kneels in the flamboyant porch with the choir of angels under a canopy of state; and balancing this apotheosis is the Mother, humanly happy in her child, against a world of natural beauty and splendour. But that child, we must not fail to notice, lies on the tattered cloth that we have seen round its loins on the cross. The cross is never wholly absent from Grünewald's vision: it throws its shadow even on the Infant, as in many of Botticelli's works.[1]

In the right wing we see the triumph of the Incarnation. The body, which was tortured into ugliness, now rises in glory. The twisting, ice-blue folds of the shroud fall away to discover the resplendent figure in scarlet and yellow, whose wounds now radiate light. The head shines at the centre of a huge aureole that works out through prismatic colours to the deep calm of the sky and its stars. Grünewald has been accused of morbidity, but if he had been morbid he could not have ended with this triumph.

[1] See Plates XXVIII, XXX and XXXIII of the *Botticelli* in this series.

But he has not, indeed, quite ended. The wings open once again (Plate x), to develop the theme quietly sounded in the first appearance of St Anthony. We see him now in his temptations and we see him in holy conversation with his fellow hermit, St Paul, in a landscape of exotic invention. It might seem strange that this should be the close—an anticlimax after the *Resurrection*. But it must be remembered that religious painters, who were not believers in art for art's sake, were primarily concerned with what, in connexion with other painters in this series, I have called the didactic pattern. As I understand it, Grünewald's intention was to show that the possibility of St Anthony's or any man's triumph is the result of Christ's enterprise, the fulfilment of what is represented in the outer panels. It might be thought that, as the altarpiece was commissioned by the Antonites, Grünewald probably had no choice: the life of St Anthony was to be the innermost display, as his statue holds the centre: but this is to ignore one of the most astonishing but also one of the commonest characteristics of the great artist— his power to profit from limitations. The most rigid terms of a commission, far from cramping an artist, often stimulate him; and where they do not exist in subject, he often creates them himself in form, as in the poet's invention of elaborately restricting metres and rhyme schemes.

Grünewald's Christ is the God of the poor and the suffering. Except for the *Resurrection*, we never see Him in splendour. The same vision that created the Crucifixions created *The Mocking of Christ* (Plate iv). He is abased, submissive, humbled even unto insult. The composition is here again very baroque. The movement in and out of space is extremely free, swirling about the still point of the central hand; and yet sufficiently controlled by the St Andrew's cross in which it is clamped together. Grünewald's discipline is shown by the way he balances the still figure of Christ in the lower left section by a similar passage of relative calm in the top right. The violence streaks across this quiet axis.

In *Christ Bearing the Cross* (Plate xxxvi) we find a Christ more positive in suffering, struggling to endure. The violence surrounding Him shows up all the more effectively for the rigid lines of the cross and spears and the calm classical background—a Renaissance influence which only occurs in one other work, *The Founding of Santa Maria Maggiore* (Plate xxxii).

I have only space to comment on one of the works not connected with the Passion—the *St Maurice and St Erasmus* (Plate xxxix). It has been much admired for its realization of plastic form and the richness of its painting, but I must confess that it has always left me uneasy. I find the figures stilted and emotionally empty, and I cannot help feeling that its fame is largely the result of that school of criticism which automatically hailed a technical advance as a mark of advancing genius. But to-day we know that technical advance may accompany spiritual decline; and for me this late and masterly piece of painting marks the fading from Grünewald's spirit of the vision and the passion which had made his earlier work so tremendous and so rare. For surely there is no painter whose work is so profound an expression of the perennial conflict between matter and spirit, science and faith, death and resurrection; or who has so far succeeded in talking two languages at once, the language of medical and psychological diagnosis and the language of metaphysical wisdom.

References. My chief authority has been Burkhard. The Sandrart quotation is from *Teutsche Academie der Edlen Bau-, Bild- und Mahlerey-Künste*, Vol. I, 1675, Vol. II, 1679; the Spengler from *The Decline of the West*, VII, viii; and the Auden from the first poem in *Look, Stranger*.

Notes to the Illustrations

Plates I–III.

Formerly in the church at Bindlach, near Bayreuth. Presented to Lindenhardt in 1685. Centre of altar contains wooden statues of the Virgin and saints; and the insides of the wings carved reliefs of two saints and the Emperor Henry and Empress Kunigunde. The date is carved on the frame and therefore presumed to be that of the painting.

Plate IV.

First attributed to Grünewald in 1909. The man in a turban, who seems to plead for mercy, has been interpreted as Joseph of Arimathea.

Plates V and VI.

Probably upper portions of the fixed wings of Dürer's Heller Altarpiece, painted for the Dominican Church in Frankfort-on-Main, and mostly destroyed by fire in the seventeenth century. It was dated 1509. St Cyrian is exorcising the daughter of Diocletian. Inscription on book: AVCTORITATE DOMINI NOSTRI JESV CHRISTI EXORCEO TE.

Plate VII.

Burkhard dates as 'not much after 1505'. Inscription between head and raised arm of centurion: VERE FILIVS DEI ERAT ILLE (Truly this was the son of God: Matt. xxviii. 54). Nothing is known of the picture's history: it first appears in the inventory of the Basle collection in 1775.

Plates VIII–XXX.

Ordered by Abbot Guido Guersi for the monastery of St Anthony at Isenheim, near Colmar. It was completed by the time of his death in 1516. The superstructure and some of the carved figures were burnt for firewood and the whole altar barely escaped destruction at the time of the French Revolution. The carvings had been ordered by Guersi's predecessor, Jean d'Orliac. It has been suggested that the St Anthony of St Anthony and St Paul the Hermit is a portrait of Guersi, because his arms are depicted on a small shield in the left foreground; but this is not now accepted. The following inscriptions appear:

By St John the Baptist in the Crucifixion: ILLVM OPORTET CRESCERE MF AVTEM MINVI (He must increase but I must decrease: John iii. 30).

13

In the open book in the *Annunciation*: ECCE VIRGO CONCIPIET ET PARIET FILIVM (Behold a virgin shall conceive and bear a son: Isaiah viii. 14). The figure of Isaiah is in the top left corner.

On a parchment in the right corner of *The Temptation of St Anthony*: VBI ERAS JESV BONE VBI ERAS QVARE NON AFFVISTI SANARES VULNERA MEA (Where wert thou, good Jesus, where wert thou? Why didst thou not come to heal my wounds?)

Plate XXXI.

An altar for the chapel of Our Lady of the Snows, in the Collegiate Church of Aschaffenburg, was completed in 1519. It is recorded as having been painted by a 'Meister Matheus'. This may have been the central panel of which the next plate was the right wing. It was first definitely attributed to Grünewald in 1907.

Plate XXXII.

See also note to last plate. On 3 August, 352, the Virgin appeared to Pope Liberius and a Roman patrician, who wished to found a church, and told them that it should be built on the Esquiline Hill on a site marked by a fall of snow. They found the isolated patch of snow. The ground was immediately consecrated and the church of Our Lady of the Snows, now Santa Maria Maggiore, was built. The Pope is shown in the act of consecration, a part of which consisted of digging three holes. The patrician and his wife are seen kneeling beyond. In the left background the Pope is dreaming (the building is a wing of the Lateran Palace), while the patrician and his wife sit on the steps and gaze up at the Virgin, who appears at the top right, above the old Lateran basilica.

Plate XXXIII.

Found in the Rhineland in 1922 and now almost universally accepted as the 'small crucifixion' referred to by Sandrart as belonging to William the Pious of Bavaria. Nearly a dozen early copies exist. The date is much discussed, some authorities placing it before the Basle *Crucifixion* and others as contemporary with that of Karlsruhe.

Plates XXXIV and XXXVI.

These panels were the front and reverse of an altarpiece in the village church of Tauberbischofsheim. The *Crucifixion* was recognized by the painter Hans

Thoma, in 1873. It was acquired by the Kassel Art Gallery in 1882 and a year later, during restoration, the *Christ Bearing the Cross* was identified. The panel was sawn apart so that both sides could be displayed at once. It was returned to Tauberbischofsheim in 1889 and acquired by Karlsruhe in 1899. Inscription on building in Plate XXXVI: ER. IST. VMB. VNSER. SVND. WILLEN. GESCLAGEN (He was wounded for our transgressions: Isaiah liii. 5).

Plate XXXIX.

St Erasmus, who carries a windlass, the instrument of his torture, is believed to be a portrait of Cardinal Albrecht von Brandenburg. The arms on his alb are those of three German bishoprics. St Maurice was the Egyptian leader of the Theban legion. There is no authority, even in legend, for their meeting. In 1525 the picture belonged to the Collegiate Church at Halle.

Plates XLI–XLVIII.

Attempts have been made to date Grünewald's drawings, but they are not satisfactory. Where it is accepted that a drawing relates to a known painting, dating is, of course, possible: but these relationships themselves are sometimes questioned. I have therefore omitted all dates and only made tentative suggestions of relationship.

Plate XLII.

Various interpretations have been placed on this drawing: as representing the diabolic trinity, pride and the lusts of the eyes and of the flesh; the *philosophia triplex*, reason, nature and morality; Dialectic, Philosophy and Theology; or as the three steps to wisdom, *studiosus*, *melancholicus* and *senex*. I am inclined to doubt whether it matters.

Plate XLVI.

The inscription reads: 'Disses hatt Mathis von Ossenburg des Churfürst(n) v. Mentz Moler gemacht vnd wo du Mathis GeSchriben findest das hat Er Mit Eigner Handt gemacht'. To the left, (M)*athis* is signed in the same hand, (incorrectly transcribed by another hand as *Matsia*). If we were certain that this is in Grünewald's hand, it would help, for it reads, in English: This was made by Matthias of Aschaffenburg, painter to the Elector of Mainz, and where you find Mathis written, that did he make with his own hand.

I. ST GEORGE AND
OTHER SAINTS. Left
wing of Lindenhardt
Altar. 1503. Pine.
160×69 cm. Linden-
hardt, near Bayreuth,
Parish Church. The attri-
bution of this altar to
Grünewald, first made in
1915, is generally, but not
universally, accepted.

II. ST DENIS AND OTHER SAINTS. Right wing of Lindenhardt Altar. See opposite plate. Fourteen saints altogether are represented. They were the helpers in time of need.

III. THE MAN OF SORROWS. Back of the centre of the Lindenhardt Altar.
159 × 153 cm. See Plate I and Notes to the Illustrations.

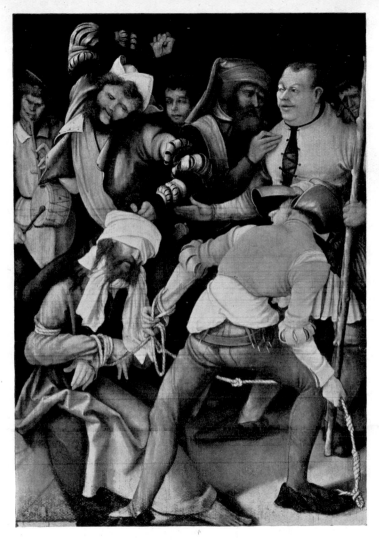

IV. THE MOCKING OF CHRIST. C. 1505. Pine. 107×72 cm. Munich,
Alte Pinakothek. See Notes to the Illustrations.

S · CIRIACVS

V. ST CYRIAC. 1511–13. Pine. 99×43 cm. Frank-fort-on-Main, Städisches Historisches Museum. See Notes to the Illustrations.

VI. ST LAWRENCE.
Signed with monogram:
M. G. N. Companion
panel to opposite plate.
Both are painted in
grisaille, with a few notes
of black and yellow.

S · LAVRENCIVS ·

VII. THE CRUCIFIXION. Before 1508. Linden. 75×55 cm. Basle,
Öffentlichesammlung. See Notes to the Illustrations.

VIII. THE ISENHEIM ALTAR. Before 1516. Wings closed. Panels and details are reproduced in Plates XI–XVIII. Linden. Colmar, Unterdenlinden Museum. See Notes to the Illustrations.

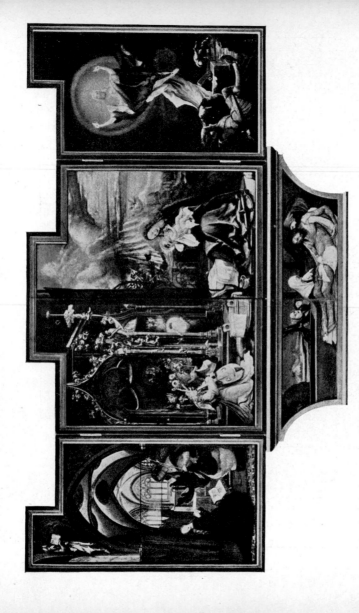

IX. THE ISENHEIM ALTAR. Outer wings open. Panels and details are reproduced in Plates XIX–XXIV. See Plate VIII.

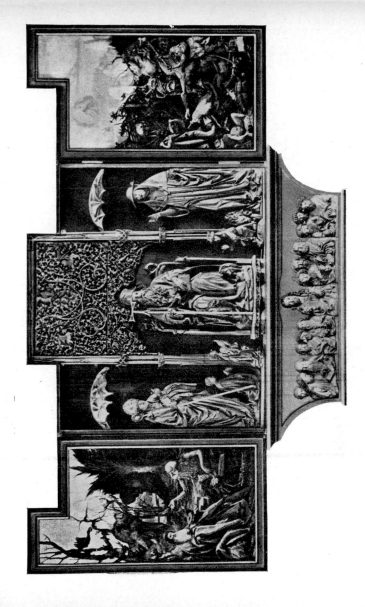

X. THE ISENHEIM ALTAR. Inner wings open. Panels and details are reproduced in Plates XXV–XXX. The carvings depict St Anthony, by the Alsatian Nikolaus von Hagenau, flanked by Sts Augustine and Jerome, perhaps also by him. The predella, depicting Christ flanked by the Apostles, is by Sebastian Beychel.

XI. THE CRUCIFIXION. Centre panel of Plate VIII. 269×307 cm.

XII. (*Opposite*) Detail of above plate.

XIII. THE VIRGIN MARY AND ST JOHN THE EVANGELIST. Detail from Plate XI.

XIV. ST JOHN THE BAPTIST. Detail from Plate XI.

XV. Details from Plate
XI.

XVI. Details from Plate
XI.

XVII. ST ANTHONY. Left
fixed wing from Plate VIII.
332×75 cm.

XVIII. ST SEBASTIAN.
Right fixed wing from Plate
VIII. 332×76 cm. For detail
see Frontispiece.

XIX. THE INCARNATION. Centre panel of Plate IX. 265 × 304 cm.

XX. (*Opposite*) CHOIR OF ANGELS. Detail from above plate.

XXI. VIRGIN AND CHILD. Detail from Plate XIX.

XXII. ANGELS AND SHEPHERDS. Detail from Plate XIX.

XXIV. THE RESURRECTION.
Right wing of Plate IX. 269 × 143 cm.

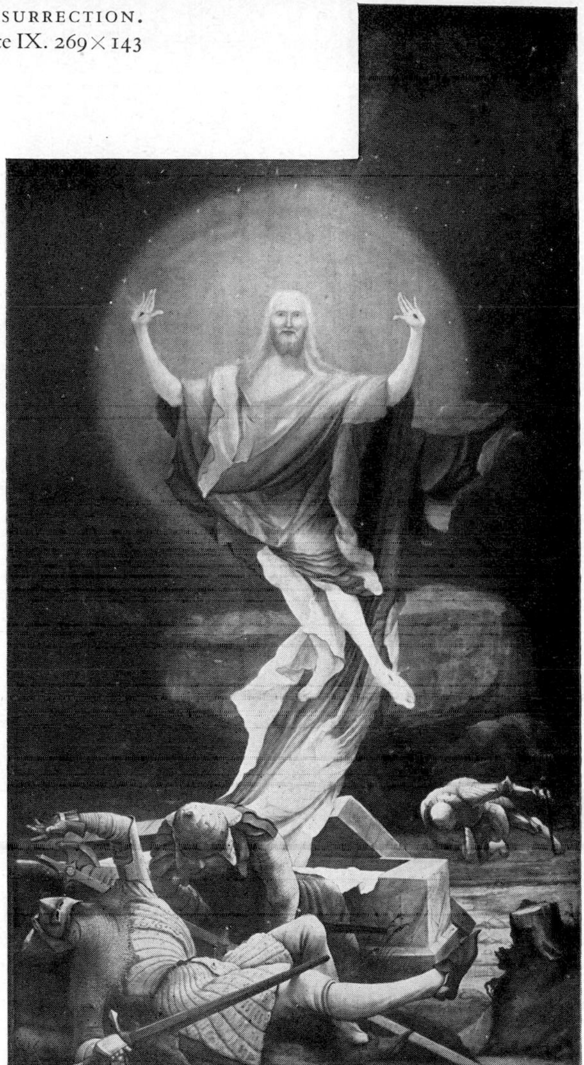

XXVII. ST PAUL THE HERMIT. Detail of Plate XXV.

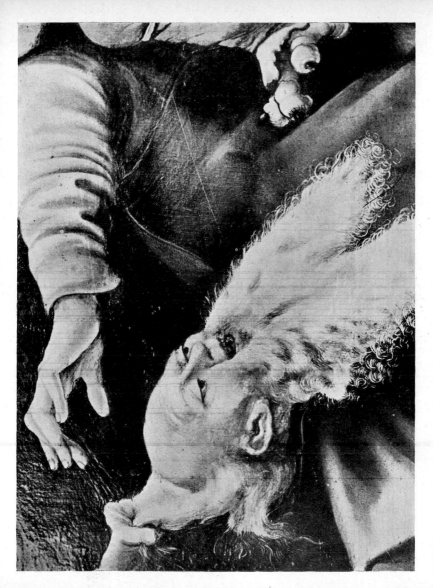

XXVIII. ST ANTHONY. Detail of Plate XXVI

XXIX. Detail of Plate XXVI.

XXXI. THE STUPPACH MADONNA. 1519. Pine. 187×146 cm. Stuppach, near Mergentheim, Parish Church. See Notes to the Illustrations.

XXII. THE FOUNDING OF
ANTA MARIA MAGGIORE
519. Pine. 179 × 92 cm. Freiburg
Breisgau, Municipal Art Gal-
ry. See Notes to the Illustrations.

XXXIII. THE CRUCIFIXION, known as THE SMALL CRUCIFIXION. ? 1519–20.
Linden. 62 × 46 cm. Haarlem, Coll. Franz Koenigs. See Notes to the Illustrations.

XXXIV. THE CRUCIFIXION. 1522–3. Pine. 196×153 cm. Karlsruhe, Kunsthalle.
See Notes to the Illustrations, and Plates XXXV and XLIV.

XXXV. ST JOHN THE EVANGELIST. Detail of Plate XXXIV.

XXXVI. (*Opposite*) CHRIST CARRYING THE CROSS. 1522–3. Originally
reverse of Plate XXXIV. (See Notes to the Illustrations.) Karlsruhe, Kunsthalle.

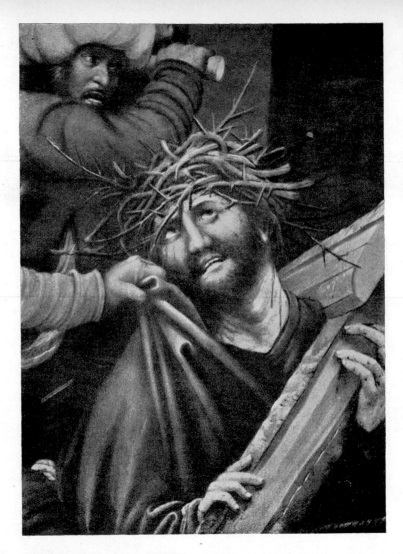

XXXVII. Detail of Plate XXXVI.

XXXVIII. Detail of Plate XXXVI.

XXXIX. THE MEETING OF ST MAURICE AND ST ERASMUS. ? 1523.
Linden. 226 × 176 cm. Munich, Alte Pinakothek. See Notes to the Illustrations.

XL. Detail of opposite plate.

XLI. ST DOROTHEA. Black crayon, heightened with white. 35·8×25·6 cm.
Berlin, Kupferstichkabinett. Perhaps study for a lost picture of the Virgin
and female saints in Mainz Cathedral, painted in 1520.

XLII. THREE MEN'S HEADS. Signed with monogram: M. G. Black crayon.
27·2 × 19·9 cm. Berlin, Kupferstichkabinett. See Notes to the Illustrations.

XLIII. WOMAN WITH FOLDED HANDS. Black crayon. 38·4 × 28·3 cm.
Lützschena, Coll. Freiherr Speck von Sternburg.

XLIV. MAN WITH FOLDED HANDS. Black crayon. 43·4 × 32 cm. Berlin, Kupferstichkabinett. Probably study for St John in Plate XXXIV.

XLV. KNEELING APOSTLE. (? St Peter.) Black crayon, heightened with white. 14·8 × 26·3 cm. Dresden, Kupferstichkabinett. Probably study for a lost *Transfiguration*, reported to have been in the Dominican Church at Frankfort-on-Main.

XLVI. WOMAN WITH FOLDED HANDS. Black crayon. 38×24
cm. Oxford, University College. See Notes to the Illustrations.

XLVII. HEAD OF A SMILING WOMAN. Black crayon. 20·1 × 14·7 cm. Paris, Louvre.
XLVIII. (*Opposite*) HEAD OF A WOMAN. Black crayon. 27·6 × 19·6 cm. Berlin, Kupferstichkabinett.

Biographical Notes

c. 1475   Born, probably in Würzburg.
Before 1504–1519.   In Seligenstadt and member of Guild.
1508–1514. Court painter to Archbishop of Mainz, Uriel von Gemmingen.
After 1514–1526.   Court painter to Archbishop Albrecht von Brandenburg.
Active for a time in Aschaffenburg, where he played some part in work on the castle. Designed a fireplace and fountains. May have been in Alsace.
1528.   Died before 1 September in Halle. He left an adopted son.

Bibliographical Notes

Burkhard, Arthur. *Mathias Grünewald. Personality and Accomplishment.* Harvard University Press, 1936. The only general work on Grünewald in English. It is fully illustrated and well documented. It gives references to earlier bibliographies and seventeen pages of bibliography of 'the most important published works' since 1914. The great majority are in German. Attention may be drawn to the following French work of critical, but not scholarly, value:

Huysmans, J. K. *Trois Eglises et Trois Primitifs.*

We would also draw attention to the following publications since Burkhard:

Schoenberger, Guido. *The Drawings of Mathis Gothart Nithart Called Gruenwald.* New York, 1948. A handsome volume with an English text.

Zervos, Christian. *Grünewald's Isenheimer Altar.* Paris, 1936. A folding plate shows the arrangement of the whole altar, and thirty-one other plates illustrate details. Preface in French.

There is no general history of German art in English but the following in German can be recommended:

Glaser, Curt. *Die Altdeutscher Malerei.* Munich, 1924.